"We all love a happy [...] This short, engag[...] surprising book shows you how you can find yours. This will help you see Easter—and life—in a whole new way."

REBECCA MANLEY PIPPERT, Speaker; Author, *Out of the Saltshaker* and *LiveGrowKnow* DVD curriculum

"A great little book to give away at Easter. Everyone longs for a happy ending in life, and Jonty unpacks the Bible's answer with warmth and clarity."

MATT FULLER, Senior Minister, Christ Church Mayfair; Author, *Perfect Sinners* and *Be True to Yourself*

"We all love a story with a happy ending, because we all long for happy endings in our own lives. In this clear, compelling, creative and concise book, Jonty Allcock shows that only Jesus can bring us the happy ending we need because he has smashed death by his own death and resurrection. All who read this book will discover the truth, wonder and significance of the Easter story afresh, and find the hope and happy ending they crave."

JOHN STEVENS, National Director, Fellowship of Independent Evangelical Churches (FIEC)

"'They think it's all over... It is now!' The greatest stories in history often come with a double ending. Jesus' story is no different, and nor is ours. In this beautiful little book, Jonty Allcock shows how Jesus offers us a glorious Sunday ending to wipe away the pain of our inevitable Friday ending, if we will accept it. A simple but ingenious analogy to help explain the story of Easter and salvation."

JENNIE POLLOCK, Writer and editor

JONTY ALLCOCK

HAPPILY EVER AFTER

HOW EASTER CAN CHANGE
YOUR LIFE FOR GOOD

thegoodbook
COMPANY

Happily Ever After
© Jonty Allcock 2020

Published by:
The Good Book Company

thegoodbook.com | www.thegoodbook.co.uk
thegoodbook.com.au | thegoodbook.co.nz | thegoodbook.co.in

ISBN: 9781784984717 | Printed in India

Design by André Parker

Contents

Contents

The Power of an Ending

Endings have great power. A good one leaves you deeply satisfied and joyful. It just feels so right. But a bad one can leave you frustrated and disappointed. It wasn't supposed to end this way.

I learned this the hard way.

It was school sports day, and I was about to run in my first ever race: a 60m sprint. I was six years old, and to be honest I made a really good start. By the halfway point (to my great surprise and joy), I was quite a long way ahead. My legs were pumping, my arms were flying and my heart was pounding.

It was an amazing feeling.

But then I noticed something suspicious ahead of me. Two adults were standing at the end with a ribbon right across where I was about to run. What was that about?

Were they trying to trip me up as I finished? I wasn't going to fall for that sort of trick—so I ran right up to the ribbon and then stopped. Just before it.

I raised my hands in triumph and turned around just in time to see all the others kids rush past me. I came last.

A great start. A strong middle. But a disastrous ending.

When my mum tried to console me by reminding me of my great start, it didn't help. When she assured me that I was fastest through the middle section, I didn't care. The ending was all that mattered—and that had been a disaster.

Thirty years on I think I've recovered from that moment—but this pattern is repeated over and over in our lives.

Our lives are made up of a series of mini-stories, each with their own mini-ending. And these stories then weave together to make up the one big story of our lives, which builds towards one ultimate ending.

"The End" has great power.

We hope for happy endings for ourselves and for those we love. We go to a friend's wedding, celebrate their love and hope they will live happily ever after. We watch our favourite sports team, get more and more excited as they get through each round, and shout with delight when they win the cup.

Some happy endings are small—you get to the baker's just in time to buy the last doughnut. Others are bigger—your house renovation is finished after six months of chaos and dust. And some are lifelong—the safe birth of a much longed-for child.

Some endings are really, really good simply because the starting point was really, really bad. Sometimes it is only the thought of the ending that gives hope...

FAIRYTALES

This is what makes fairytales so enduringly popular. They take you on a journey from darkness to light; from night to day; from sorrow to joy. They're based on the idea of a hope-creating ending.

You read them with this sense of security: no matter what terrible disasters befall the characters, it will all be ok in the end.

You're waiting for the moment when everyone lives happily ever after and the hope that has been building comes to pass.

The deeper the sorrow—the brighter the joy; the harder the battle—the sweeter the victory.

These are the sorts of endings we look for in stories: endings that make sense of all the mayhem that has come before.

These sorts of perfect endings resonate with something deep within us.

HOPE-CREATING

Every parent who has taken their children on a long car journey has tasted this. The repeated question from the back seat is "Are we there yet?" That's a question that expresses a deep and profound longing for "The End".

I find it hard to be patient with that question. When it's asked for the hundredth time in the space of ten minutes, I find it hard not to become sarcastic. "No darling, the car is still moving at seventy mph along the motorway. It really is unbelievably obvious that we're not there yet. You will know we are there because we will stop. I will turn off the engine and say, 'We're here'. Why don't we wait for that moment?"

"OK... but are we there yet?"

It's deeply annoying on a car journey, but it's a question we never stop asking. As situations arise and struggles come our way, we find ourselves asking, "Are we there yet?"

We may not be entirely sure where "there" is, but we know that "here" is hard and "there" is better, and so we long for an end of "here" and our arrival at "there".

Endings have great power. A good one leaves you deeply satisfied and joyful. It just feels so right.

HOW LONG?

In the Bible there's a version of this question. You find it in several places, and it's beautifully honest: *How long?*

> *How long must I wrestle with my thoughts*
>   *and day after day have sorrow in my heart?*
>   *How long will my enemy triumph over me?*
>
> *Psalm 13 verse 2*

Here's someone who's in a place of sorrow and struggle, and they're longing for it to come to an end.

Sometimes it's only the thought of an ending that enables us to keep walking through the rain. These are the endings that are precious to us. The clouds break and the sun comes out and the pain is over. Finally over.

NOT JUST HAPPY ENDINGS

But of course, not all endings are happy endings—not in films, not in books and not in life. Some endings have the power to take something good and completely ruin it. This is when endings are at their most destructive. They can crush dreams, shatter hopes and mock our ambitions.

Maybe you can think of some endings like that in your own life. Your job was great—until they made you redundant. Your holiday was perfect—until you broke your leg. Your relationship was for life—until she found someone else.

"The End" casts its shadow over our lives. When things are good, we desperately try to act as if there's no end coming. We scrunch up our eyes and try to live in the moment. We're told to capture the present and enjoy every second. We live in a culture that idolises "now" and suppresses any thought of an end. This is some of what lies behind the trend towards "mindfulness", encouraging us to live in and enjoy the present.

I'm sure that there are some benefits in the advice to slow down and be more intentional, but every tick of the clock, every setting of the sun, and every church bell that rings tells us the same story: the end is coming. Time is like sand running through our fingers—and when you stop to think about it, that can be terrifying.

There is a short poem by the hymnwriter Henry Twells, engraved on a clock in Chester Cathedral, that says:

> When as a child I laughed and wept, time crept.
> When as a youth I waxed more bold, time strolled.
> When I became a full-grown man, time ran.
> When older still I daily grew, time flew.
> Soon I shall find, in passing on, time gone.

It speaks of the relentless and unstoppable march of the end. The closer it gets, the faster it seems to come. In some ways this may seem gloomy, but there's no point in trying pretend that it's not this way.

Every single thing in this world has an end. Everything has a "Best before" date. Nothing lasts for ever.

The Bible tells it straight. It's not a book of sickly sweet slogans that aren't true. It's realistic and honest about the world we live in. Look at what a man called James says:

> *What is your life? You are a mist that appears for a little while and then vanishes.*   *James 4 v 14*

In another part of the Bible, we read this blunt assessment of human life:

> *Surely the fate of human beings is like that of the animals; the same fate awaits them both: as one dies, so dies the other. All have the same breath; humans have no advantage over animals. Everything is meaningless.*   *Ecclesiastes 3 v 19*

Here lie the greatest kingdoms, the strongest empires, the most powerful dynasties. All of them swept aside by "The End".

Human history is punctuated by these two little words. There is no hero, no king, no warrior and no billionaire that can withstand their approach. They can sometimes be postponed but can never be cancelled. In "The End", these are the last words on every human story.

The words of James and Ecclesiastes, quoted above, aren't written in the Bible so that we all become despairing. They're calling us to wake up and see reality.

Our stories will come to an end. Many choose to ignore that—but is that really wise? Perhaps true wisdom, and the perfect ending we seek, is not found by ignoring the reality of our end but by embracing and understanding it more carefully.

OUR STORY

The great question of life is not "Will it end?" (We know it will.) But will it have a good ending or a bad one, a sad ending or a happy ending?

We know that life isn't actually a fairytale—and in our own lives we may have found that happy endings are rarer than sad endings. And even our happiest endings aren't "ever after", because we know that the ultimate end is coming—the end of life.

Will that be happy? Or sad?

In order to try and find answers, I'd like to take you back 2,000 years and to events that took place in a distant land. At first sight it may seem that this has nothing to do with us—but the connections we'll discover run deeper than you know.

The events of the very first Easter hold the key to how our own story ends. As we'll see—Easter really can change your life for good.

Jesus' Friday Ending

Do you have a favourite story? Maybe it's a book you've read many times, or a film you've seen so often that you can quote the best lines. Perhaps it's an epic television series that you binge-watched over a weekend. It may even be a real-life story about someone you know.

In many ways the story of Jesus is very ordinary. It's the story of a baby born into a poor working-class family. It's the story of an ordinary boy growing up in the home of an ordinary carpenter. It's the story of an ordinary man living in an ordinary town.

But the story of Jesus is the most *extraordinary* story ever told. It's recorded for us in the Bible in four eye-witness accounts. We can read them in the Gospels of Matthew, Mark, Luke and John, who carefully researched the story and wrote it down so that we could know it.

For the sake of time and space, let's cut right to the end of the Jesus story. After all, that's what we're particularly interested in. How did his story end? And what might that have to do with us?

A DOUBLE ENDING

When you skip forward to the end of his life, you discover a double ending. The story of Jesus ends twice—and these two endings perfectly fit with the two types of endings we saw in chapter 1: either hope-destroying or hope-creating.

The first ending happened on a Friday. That was the day when Jesus—having been betrayed, mocked and beaten—was hung up on a Roman cross to die. That was his Friday Ending. It was a hope-destroying end that left a young man cut down in his prime.

It was definitely an end, but it was not "The End" for Jesus. Three days later, on a bright Sunday morning, Jesus walked out of the grave, alive again. This was his Sunday Ending. Here was a hope-creating ending of breathtaking beauty and power.

Friday Ending. Sunday Ending. We need to look carefully at both of these to see what actually happened, before we then look for the connection to ourselves.

So, come back with me through 2,000 years of history and watch as Jesus meets his Friday End.

FRIDAY

Here's how the story of Jesus ended on the day we call Good Friday. He was hanging on a cross; nails had been driven through his hands and his feet; he was gasping for air—and then it was all over.

With a loud cry, Jesus breathed his last.

Mark 15 v 37

It was all taken away in that moment. Just eight words. It's not dressed up in flowery and fancy language. Instead, it's brutal and devastating. He took a final breath, and he was gone.

Death has a habit of doing that: like an unwelcome guest, like a thoughtless intruder. It just barges its way in and brings things to a sudden and tragic end. Although this happened a long time ago in a place that's far away, we need to feel how wrong this ending is.

This isn't a satisfying conclusion. And when you begin to look more closely at the life of Jesus, it becomes even more clear that this was a terrible and hope-destroying end.

Here are three reasons why the death of Jesus was a terrible end to his extraordinary life. It seems so unfair, so futile and so final.

UNFAIR

We might be used to seeing churches with a cross at the front—perhaps even with a figure of Jesus still nailed there—but have you ever stopped to think about how he ended up dying that way?

The cross was a form of execution used by the Romans as punishment for the very worst of criminals: murderers, traitors and the like.

How did a humble carpenter from the small town of Nazareth come to end up on a cross?

It certainly wasn't because he deserved it. Jesus wasn't being punished for anything he'd done wrong—that much is very obvious. The Roman governor, Pontius Pilate, who examined the evidence, concluded this:

I have found in him no grounds for the death penalty.
Luke 23 v 22

The charges that were brought against Jesus were all lies. He was wrongly accused, wrongly arrested and wrongly convicted. Yet the angry crowd demanded his death.

In fact, we can go further. Not only had Jesus not committed a crime but, as you read the accounts of his life, you discover that he never did *anything* wrong. Here was the perfectly innocent man. No one else can claim that except Jesus. Every thought, every word and every deed was perfect.

The guilty man
went free, and the
innocent man was
handed over to death.

This is the sort of
ending that we hate.

Why was Jesus perfectly innocent? He looked like an ordinary man. He may even have looked like any other criminal. But Jesus wasn't just a man. The Bible tells us that he was God's own Son: he was completely human— but also completely divine and perfectly pure.

Jesus' perfection pointed to his identity as God's Son— and the things Jesus did proved that identity. Again and again he did things that only God can do, such as healing the sick with a touch, calming a storm with a word, and even bringing someone back to life. (You can read about these things in Mark 1 v 40-42; 4 v 35-41 and 5 v 35-43.)

One of the criminals crucified with Jesus saw his innocence clearly. Listen to his comment:

> We are getting what our deeds deserve. But this man
> has done nothing wrong.   Luke 23 v 41

It's crystal clear that Jesus died as an innocent man. There was no justice here. He was lied about in the Jewish court, he was battered by the Roman guards, he was mocked by the religious leaders, and he was condemned by the angry crowd. Do you feel that injustice? It's a terrible end to a life.

There *was* a guilty man that day—his name was Barabbas. He really was a criminal, and he was facing death on a cross. But when given the choice, the crowd chose to set Barabbas free and condemn Jesus to death.

The guilty man went free, and the innocent man was handed over to death.

This is the sort of ending that we hate. And it gets worse...

FUTILE

Jesus' death really seems to be completely pointless. It was hardly a heroic and glorious death. Some stories end with the hero going to their death in a blaze of glory. Although it might be sad, that can be a satisfying end and create hope out of the tragedy. But not here: not with Jesus. It seems that he went down in a whimper of shame.

To be crucified was a humiliating way to die. It was a public, shameful and terrible death. It was designed to expose the criminal and leave their reputation in tatters. There was no attempt to preserve dignity or privacy. No one was ever impressed by a crucified corpse.

On top of that and even worse, the Jews understood from their Scriptures that anyone who was hung up on a cross was under God's curse. Here's what is written in the Old Testament book of Deuteronomy:

> *You must not leave the body hanging on the pole overnight. Be sure to bury it that same day, because anyone who is hung on a pole is under God's curse.*
> *Deuteronomy 21 v 23*

No one was impressed by this act of heroism. Jesus died alone, ashamed and cursed by God.

This was hardly the feel-good ending that Hollywood loves. This was a futile end that seems such a waste. Surely he had so much more to teach the world, so much more he could have done. His life was cut short in a futile act of violence and jealousy.

The Friday Ending of Jesus is a terrible ending. It seems unfair, it seems futile—and it seems so final...

FINAL

As Jesus died, all the hope surrounding him died with him. He had only been in the public eye for about three years, but in that time he'd really got a bit of a movement going. He had spoken of a kingdom; he had spoken about life and joy and freedom. It was a powerful message, and it was backed up with powerful miracles.

There were crowds who followed him; there were people who shouted for him; there was hope rising. Could it be that this man really was the one who could bring real change?

But the final breath of Jesus meant that all of that hope evaporated.

You catch a sense of that from a couple of his friends who watched his Friday Ending. Here's what they said:

We had hoped that he was the one who was going to redeem Israel.   *Luke 24 v 21*

"We had hoped..." Words that speak of shattered dreams. Not any more. With the final breath of Jesus, all that hope disappeared down the plughole.

Another false dawn. Another disappointment. Another human story ending in tragedy.

THE STONE

Death is final. All that was left of Jesus was a corpse. He was taken down from the cross, and his lifeless body slumped to the ground. He was wrapped in cloth and put in a tomb. Then a huge stone was placed at the entrance to the tomb.

That stone was like death itself. It rolled into place and marked the end. It shut out the light and left the body in darkness. It shut out the world and left the body alone. As the stone crashed into place, death claimed its victory. There was no coming back from this.

That was his Friday Ending. Unfair; futile; final.

In any other story that would be the end but not here: not for Jesus.

The darkness of his Friday Ending gave way to the beauty of his Sunday Ending...

Jesus' Sunday Ending

If the story of Jesus had ended on Friday, it would be a terrible story. Just another tragedy. Death has its latest victim, and hope has once again been snuffed out.

But Friday was followed by Sunday—and Sunday brought a very different ending.

It all started with the enormous stone that on Friday had been rolled into place in front of his tomb and had shut Jesus in for ever.

THE STONE

On the following Sunday morning, we're told that a group of women went to the tomb where the body of Jesus lay. The stone was very much on their minds. They wanted to anoint the body of Jesus with spices and perfume, but listen to what they were saying to one another:

Very early on the first day of the week, just after sunrise, they were on their way to the tomb and they asked each other, "Who will roll the stone away from the entrance of the tomb?"   Mark 16 v 2-3

"Who will roll the stone away?" (This is a great question—remember it for later.)

The women were clearly expecting that the tomb would be as it was on Friday. The stone would still be in place, arrogantly declaring that death had won.

They understood that death is "The End". It is the full stop at the end of a life, and there's no coming back. Everyone knows that. Death is a one-way street. The stone only rolls in one direction.

But when they arrived at the grave, here's what they found:

But when they looked up, they saw that the stone, which was very large, had been rolled away.

Mark 16 v 4

When I grew up, watching a film meant getting it on video. At the end of the film, you had to remember to rewind the videotape ready for the next time it was to be watched. It was mildly amusing if you watched as the tape reversed, as you could view the film in high-speed reverse and see the story undoing itself.

That's what's happening here. Things are happening in reverse. The stone that represents death itself has now been rolled away.

The women were getting the very first glimpse of the Sunday ending. But they didn't understand it yet.

THE ANNOUNCEMENT

With the stone removed, the women could enter the tomb to go and find the body. But rather than finding Jesus, they were confronted with a young man dressed in a white robe, who gave them this message:

> *You are looking for Jesus the Nazarene, who was*
> *crucified. He has risen!*   Mark 16 v 6

Here is their second glimpse of the Sunday Ending. "He has risen!" It was the last thing they were expecting to hear—but if those words are true, they change everything.

The women still didn't understand what they were seeing. In fact, their first reaction to the stone and the announcement shows what shock they were in:

> *Trembling and bewildered, the women went out and*
> *fled from the tomb. They said nothing to anyone,*
> *because they were afraid.*   Mark 16 v 8

This is not a warm and fluffy ending where everyone smiles and feels good. They weren't dealing with a sentimental fairy story. They were presented with hard facts that shook the very foundation of their world.

No one had imagined this. No one had expected this. How could this possibly be true?

THE APPEARING

To put matters beyond any doubt, Jesus appeared to the women in person.

> *Suddenly Jesus met them. "Greetings," he said. They came to him, clasped his feet and worshipped him. Then Jesus said to them, "Do not be afraid. Go and tell my brothers to go to Galilee; there they will see me."*
>
> *Matthew 28 v 9-10*

Can you even begin to imagine that moment? The confusion, the questions, the hope, the joy? Here is the great Sunday Ending of Jesus.

The body that on Friday had breathed its last was now breathing again. The heart that had stopped beating on Friday was pumping again. The eyes that had closed in death had now opened again to the bright light of a new day.

He was alive again. And all the pain and sorrow of Friday dissolved away in the fresh Sunday sunshine of Easter morning.

Death is like a large stone that rolls into place and cannot be moved. But Jesus rolled death backwards. He reversed it.

Jesus spent forty more days on earth, appearing to over five hundred different people. He wanted to leave the world in no doubt that he really was alive again. And at the end of those forty days he was taken up to heaven.

Now here's an ending worth getting excited about. If Friday felt like a terrible end, then Sunday feels so right.

But this is more than just a happy ending. It's an ending that declares two important things about Jesus.

HIS VICTORIOUS ENDING

Until that Sunday morning, death had had a monopoly on endings. But in that moment, death was upstaged and exposed. Death lost it's 100% record, and had to give up its unique claim on the words "The End".

We must see the bigness of what was happening here. Here is a glimmer of hope that maybe death might not have to be the end of the story.

Death is like a large stone that rolls into place and cannot be moved. But Jesus rolled death backwards. He reversed it.

What happened that weekend 2,000 years ago was an epic battle. Two powerful enemies went to war. Death on one side: an undefeated champion. Jesus on the other side. It was a vicious fight, and on Friday it looked to all the world as if Death had won.

Until Sunday morning.

Here's a sentence from the Bible that sums up how the battle went down:

Christ Jesus ... has destroyed death and has brought life and immortality to light through the gospel.
2 Timothy 1 v 10

That is the simple summary of how the battle went. Jesus didn't just about scrape through; he didn't narrowly win. He *destroyed* death. It was a victory, and it was decisive, complete and absolute.

Death tried its best—but ended up the loser.

Another part of the Bible puts it like this:

It was impossible for death to keep its hold on him.
Acts 2 v 24

No matter how hard Death tried, it just couldn't hold on. For the first time ever, Death was in trouble. There was something about this man that was unlike any other man that death has ever battled against. Jesus was much too powerful.

Make no mistake about it: Sunday was the day of victory.

And because Jesus defeated death, it means that this Sunday Ending never ends.

HIS FOREVER ENDING

You sometimes hear stories of people who have amazing recoveries, such as the soccer player Fabrice Muamba. In March 2012, he suffered a cardiac arrest while playing in the FA Cup quarter finals in north London. Despite his heart having stopped for 78 minutes, Muamba made a full recovery. He was brought back from the very edge of death itself.

That is what we might call *resuscitation*. And that's great in many ways. It gives people a second chance at life. But that isn't anywhere near what we're talking about here.

When someone is resuscitated, they will die again. They might have cheated death temporarily—but they haven't escaped completely.

But *resurrection* is a different thing completely. Resurrection means that Death is finished with for ever. Here's how Jesus says it in his own words:

> *I am the Living One; I was dead, and now look, I am alive for ever and ever!*   *Revelation 1 v 18*

Jesus didn't just get a few extra years of life. He rose for ever. That's what we're talking about as his Sunday Ending.

He was completely changed. He went through death to a whole new life beyond death.

Before Jesus died, his life was just like ours. He lived in this painful and decaying world. He was getting older. He knew what it was like to be hungry and tired. He experienced deep sadness, limitations, frustration, disappointment, temptation. He was part of this dying world.

Decay is part of the painful reality of our existence. Everything moves in one direction, from life towards death. It is a one-way street, and there's nothing you can do to stop it.

Jesus walked that road. He went in that direction, and it took him to his Friday End. But on Sunday all that changed. Jesus went the other way. He moved from death to life. And when he rose from the dead, he was finished with death for ever.

He was finished with decay, suffering, temptation and frustration. All of that was over, and Sunday meant a whole new life.

This is what makes Easter Sunday so good. It holds out hope of life for ever. It holds out hope of the perfect ending that we're longing for.

But this is all very well for Jesus. His Friday Ending was tragic. His Sunday Ending is great. But so what? Why should we be bothered?

That's where we're heading now. It's about to come very close to home...

Our Friday Ending

Sometimes things happen in faraway places and in distant history that have enormous implications for our lives today. This is clear to us when we consider those who gave their lives in war. We often talk about them doing it for *us*. Their sacrifice—their Friday Ending—has a direct connection to our lives now. And so we honour those sacrifices. We feel that connection.

The year 2020 is significant for many people around the world as it marks the 75th anniversary of the end of World War Two. Even all those decades later, when most of us have no direct memory of the events of the war, it matters to us that we honour those who fought for us. We feel the connection.

You may never have considered this before, but could it be that a connection also exists between our lives now and the death of Jesus on a Roman cross 2,000 years ago?

It may feel very distant and irrelevant to our lives today—but if we can begin to feel that deep connection that exists, it will start to transform our understanding of our own individual stories.

You may be a little sceptical. How can the death of Jesus have any connection to us today? Surely it's just a sad story; or perhaps an inspiring example. But the connection runs much, much deeper than that.

A DEEP CONNECTION

Jesus had a very strange view of his own Friday Ending. He talked about it as being *for* others. He didn't see his Friday Ending as a sad and tragic waste of life. Far from it. Look how he puts it in his own words:

> *Even the Son of Man* [this is how Jesus referred to himself] *did not come to be served, but to serve, and to give his life as a ransom for many.*
>
> Mark 10 v 45

Jesus was very clear in what he said. He was giving his life for others. That's the language of *sacrifice*. That's the connection I'm talking about.

If someone were to die in order to save you, it would leave you with a powerful connection to that person.

I was once at a wedding and found myself a little bored during the photos (we've all been there). To pass the time, I wandered around and read some of the gravestones in the churchyard. I found one that was very moving. It was to a 16-year-old boy who died on the 1st January 1869. His name was Fredrick Dyson. It told the story of how he had been drowned while rescuing another boy from the water. And then at the bottom was a poem—only short but beautiful:

Fame, give thy silver trumpet breath,
  a hero to commend,
Who gave to the icy jaws of death
  himself to save a friend.

On that day, Fredrick Dyson was not dying. He was safe on the bank. But his friend was drowning. So he made the decision to leave the safety of dry land and jump into the freezing water. He went to the place of death in order that his friend might live.

That is sacrifice—and it creates a connection. Do you think, for the rest of his life, that the friend would ever forget what had been done for him?

The sacrificial act of Fredrick Dyson meant the friend could live. That's the sort of connection that the Friday Ending of Jesus has to us today. He said he was dying for others, so that they could live.

But who are the others—the "many"—that Jesus was talking about? How is his death connected to them? An account of another man's death will help us to find out.

HIS DEATH FOR OTHERS

Jesus once went to the funeral of one of his closest friends: a man called Lazarus. When Jesus saw the dead man's sister, we read this about him:

> *When Jesus saw her weeping, and the Jews who had come along with her also weeping, he was deeply moved in spirit and troubled.*
>
> *John 11 v 33*

Jesus saw the suffering. He did not ignore it. In fact, in a deeply profound way, Jesus entered right into that pain. Just a few sentences later we read that...

> *Jesus wept.*   *John 11 v 35*

He was crystal clear that we live in a world that is full of Friday Endings. Jesus enjoyed good things—he laughed and loved and sang—but they were only temporary. Life was only short, and then Friday would come.

Jesus experienced the same sorrow and tears that we all experience. Throughout our lives we live through many mini-Fridays. Days of intense sadness. When relationships break, when things go wrong, when sickness steals people away from us, when joyful times become painful memories of what has been lost.

No one can avoid these endings—and no one can escape the ultimate Friday Ending that will one day bring the final curtain down on our story.

Jesus lived in our world—and he knew it was dying.

Have you ever wondered why?

THE CIRCLE OF LIFE

There's a view that says death is just part of the circle of life. It's natural. It's just the way things are, and we need to learn to cope with it. But are you really happy with that?

Perhaps, if you've had a nice comfortable life and retire at 65 to spend 20 years playing golf, you might be able to cope with that. But what about the millions in poverty? What about those killed in terrible circumstances, whose lives are cut short? Are we really happy to shrug our shoulders and say that death is just the way it is?

I think it's impossible to escape the sense that death is wrong. There is something wrong here. We get angry at death; we rage at our Friday Endings; we weep as Jesus wept. When confronted with death, (in the words of the Welsh poet Dylan Thomas) we tend to want to "Rage, rage against the dying of the light."

Perhaps we need to take those feelings more seriously. Perhaps we need a different perspective. What if death feels wrong because it *is* wrong?

A BETTER WORLDVIEW

The Bible shows us a very different view of the world—a better view. It starts with showing this earth not as an accident but as a beautiful creation coming from the mind of the Creator. The Bible story starts there:

> *In the beginning God created the heavens and the*
> *earth.*   *Genesis 1 v 1*

Humanity is, then, handcrafted by God and placed at the very centre of that creation. We were designed for relationship: a relationship with one another and a deep relationship with God. A connection between Creator and creature that would sustain life and joy and freedom.

In short, we were created for a Sunday Ending. Perhaps this is why we crave these sorts of endings. It's the way we're designed.

LOST CONNECTION

But the creatures broke off the connection with their Creator. They severed the lines and preferred to go it alone. It was an act of outright defiance and bare-faced rebellion; and, as a result, the relationship was torn apart.

This is how that moment is described:

> *They exchanged the truth about God for a lie, and*
> *worshipped and served created things rather than the*
> *Creator—who is for ever praised.*   *Romans 1 v 25*

They preferred beliefs about God and themselves that made them feel important, but weren't actually real or true. They decided to seek security and fulfilment and happiness in things that God had made, instead of in knowing the God who had made them. The Bible has a simple word for this attitude: *sin*.

As a result, the Creator-creature relationship is broken. It's hard to overestimate what a serious thing this is. It had devastating consequences for the world—it's why, as we look around us, we can see so much that is beautiful and yet so much that is broken.

It had devastating consequences for humanity too. The Creator spoke his word of punishment to those who had rebelled against him:

Dust you are and to dust you will return.

Genesis 3 v 19

From that moment forward, the creatures would face a Friday Ending to their story. Death entered the world, not as a natural process but as a penalty for the sinful rebellion. Creature and Creator would be separated for ever.

And "for ever" really does mean for ever. It's not that when we die we simply stop existing. Instead, everyone lives on—so for those who have rebelled against their Creator, that means being separated from him, and from all the good things he gives, for all eternity. That's the experience that the Bible calls "hell"—an existence without hope or joy or friendship or fulfilment or fun.

The Sunday-Ending joy that we were created for became the Friday Ending that destroys everything.

The Creator was not being harsh; he was being just. His punishment is absolutely fair. Fair on those first humans and fair on us too—because we, like they, have decided to go it alone in God's world, ignoring God completely, or making up a God who is not true but who conveniently fits in with the way we want to lead our lives.

We, like the first humans, have chosen to look to things—to worship things—that aren't God, for our security and fulfilment and happiness.

Some of us choose to worship money: others sex, others experience, or career, or family, or reputation—the list is endless. And since we have chosen to live in God's world enjoying his gifts (and worshipping his gifts) but ignoring God himself, then it's perfectly just that after death we should find ourselves no longer in God's world and with none of his gifts.

This is desperately sad, and in many ways it fits with what we see around us.

What if death feels wrong because it really is wrong? This is why the world is the way it is. We are all

God had a plan—and what a plan it was. He chose to come in person. He plunged himself into this world in the most daring rescue mission that has ever been seen.

creatures who have defied our Creator. We can try to ignore that or pretend that our sin isn't serious—but every funeral, every tear, every life cut short tells us the same message. There's a serious problem. There's something wrong.

The world is dying.

But all the while the Creator was watching, and he was not finished with the world...

STEPPING DOWN

Despite the rebellion of his creatures, God had a plan— and what a plan it was. Driven by incredible love and absolute justice, God chose to do the unthinkable.

He could have stayed in heaven, where he was safe—he could have abandoned the world to the Friday Ending it deserved—but instead he did more.

He chose to come in person. God became a man. He plunged himself into this world in the most daring rescue mission that has ever been seen.

> *The true light that gives light to everyone was coming into the world. He was in the world, and though the world was made through him, the world did not recognise him.*　　　　　*John 1 v 9-10*

The One who had made the world, stepped into the world. Here is the awesome identity of Jesus.

As he looked at the world, he was looking at the world that he had created. He was looking at his creatures, and he loved them. And his plan? Simple. He became a man so that he could die for them.

Jesus was innocent. Perfect. He didn't deserve a Friday Ending. But we are guilty. We have all rebelled against our Creator. We do deserve to die.

But Jesus came to step into our place. When Jesus died on the cross, he was taking our Friday Ending. He was dying for us.

That's the connection between him and us.

REMEMBER BARABBAS

Back in chapter 2 we saw Barabbas. He was guilty and deserved to die. But Jesus died instead of Barabbas. The innocent one dies and the guilty one goes free.

For the rest of Barabbas's life on earth, there was an unbreakable connection between the death of Jesus on the cross and his own physical life. That's a picture of what Jesus was doing.

Fredrick Dyson chose to die for a friend who didn't deserve to drown. Jesus Christ chose to die for people who *did* deserve to die.

His death wasn't a tragic and terrible end. It was the most magnificent rescue you could ever imagine. When

Jesus said that he was giving his life for others, this is what he meant.

Who gets to benefit from this? Anyone!

Anyone who will recognise that they're a creature who has ignored their Creator. Anyone who knows that their relationship with God is broken. Anyone who knows that God is right to punish their sin. Anyone who knows that they're facing a Friday Ending.

Anyone who says to Jesus, "I want to be connected to you. I want your death on the cross to be *for me*."

It's possible for our Friday Ending to be taken away. And we haven't even got to chapter 5 and Sunday yet!

Our Sunday Ending

We've come a long way, but we still haven't answered the big question that we started with: is it possible that we can find the perfect ending to our story? Can we live happily ever after? Or are we just chasing futile and impossible dreams?

There's a caterpillar that provides a brilliant parable of the futility we sometimes feel about life. It's called the Woolly Bear caterpillar and it lives in the Arctic. In many ways it's pretty standard as far as caterpillars go. Except that the arctic summer is too short for the Woolly Bear caterpillar to consume all the leaves it needs to transform into a moth. So when winter comes, it crawls under a rock and freezes. Its heart stops; its blood freezes; it is essentially dead.

But in the spring it defrosts, crawls out, and continues its munching. Another summer of eating—and still it's not had enough. So it's back under the rock for another deep freeze. This happens for seven years or more.

But then one summer comes, and the caterpillar has eaten enough. This is its moment. It makes a cocoon, emerges as a moth, and flies off into the sky. But here's the brutal reality. It has three days, and then it's dead.

Seven years of eating, freezing and defrosting. Seven years of longing for the perfect ending. And then it's all over in three days. What a picture of futility.

Many of us would hopefully say that our lives are much better than that of the Woolly Bear caterpillar. But do you still find yourself asking, "Is this it?"

Even when life is good, we can find ourselves longing for something more.

Something better.

Most of us know the direction we'd like our lives to be moving in. It could be summed up as "better". It's this magical place that we'd love to get to. We're not always entirely sure how to get there, but Better-land has a powerful pull on our hearts. We're told to pursue our dreams, to change our lives, to be whatever we want to be. It's one of the great anthems of our age. "Don't settle for the life you have now; there's more. There's a better ending for you."

All of that is the pursuit of a Sunday Ending.

Some people play the national lottery, some go on TV talent shows, some emigrate overseas, some take early retirement, some buy bigger houses. Why? Because all of these things promise us Sunday.

The trouble is that Sunday is just so elusive and slippery. How do we know when we've got there? And how do we keep hold of it when we do finally arrive? We might achieve all sorts of things. We might reach our goals and realise our dreams. Or we might end up disappointed and disillusioned. Either way, none of it lasts, and it will be gone too soon.

Imagine if there really was a better ending. Not just a brief moment of satisfaction and happiness but the end of all suffering and pain. An end to all the disappointment and frustration. An end that would change our life for good. That would be worth getting excited about.

But that's just wishful thinking.

Isn't it?

A DEEPER CONNECTION

Not only is there a connection between Jesus' Friday Ending and ours: it's true about Sunday too.

How does that connection work?

Imagine an athlete competing in the Olympics. We talk about them representing their country. Even if we're sitting on the sofa eating snacks and they're the ones out sweating on the track, a connection exists. If they win, *we* win; if they lose, *we* lose. What happens to them (as our representative) also happens to us.

The Bible talks of that sort of connection when it comes to Jesus. For example, it says that...

> *through the obedience of the one man* [Jesus] *the many will be made righteous.*　　　Romans 5 v 19

In other words, a connection exists between the actions of one person and the impact on many others.

One person obeys—that's the perfect obedience of Jesus—and many benefit by being made right with God. He is the representative who acts on behalf of others.

And that principle will help us understand the sort of connection that can exist between the Sunday Ending of Jesus and the ending of our own story. What he did as he walked out of the tomb can completely transform our own ending.

His story can become our story. His Sunday can become our Sunday.

CONNECTED TO HIS VICTORIOUS ENDING

There's a famous story in the Bible of a huge enemy called Goliath, who was tormenting God's people. No one could fight him; everyone was terrified; the people were enslaved. Then a young shepherd boy called David stepped forward and said he would fight. He took his sling and killed the enemy. He won the battle on behalf of all of the people. The crowd didn't fight—but they did win. All because they were connected to the victory that David won.

That boy David grew up to be a great king. And if you follow his family line through generations and generations, you eventually reach another boy born to be King. He was born in the dark streets of Bethlehem, and he was destined to grow up to fight another vicious enemy.

Not a warrior called Goliath but a giant called Death.

Death has been the enemy of humanity ever since that first rebellion against God. No one can defeat Death; everyone is terrified; humanity is enslaved. We cannot reverse it or cure it or prevent it. Time after time, Death wins. The stone is rolled into place and simply cannot be rolled away.

But then Jesus stepped forward. He went into battle with the great enemy Death. He went to fight on our behalf. He went to fight the battle that we cannot win. It was a vicious battle that left Jesus battered and crushed. On Friday it appeared that Death had won again.

But just wait for Sunday.

As the stone was rolled back and Jesus walked out of the grave, the announcement rang out: *Death is defeated. Jesus has won.* It's a spectacular victory that declares to the world that Jesus is more powerful than death.

But here's where the connection comes. Jesus was acting as *our* representative. He was fighting the battle on behalf of others. He was fighting for you and for me. The actions of this one man have huge implications for many others.

We can't defeat death. Death is the immovable stone that no one can roll away.

Do you remember the question that the women asked on Easter Sunday morning? "Who will roll the stone away?"

It's a great question. Who will roll away the stone of our death? Who can bring us safely through death? The message of Easter Sunday is that Jesus will and can.

His victory can become our victory. We can be connected to him and know that death has lost its power over us. So look at these words, which the early Christians wrote to describe how they now thought about death:

"Death has been swallowed up in victory."

"Where, O death, is your victory?
  Where, O death, is your sting?"

Because Jesus has
smashed through
death, then so can we.
Because Jesus has life
for ever, then so can we.

The sting of death is sin, and the power of sin is the law. But thanks be to God! He gives us the victory through our Lord Jesus Christ.

1 Corinthians 15 v 54-57

Death used to have power; it used to have a sting; it used to have the victory. But it doesn't have to be that way any more. Jesus has defeated death, and now, if we're connected to Jesus, it is powerless to harm us any more.

It's possible for our lives not to end in the defeat of Friday but in the victory of Sunday.

And Sunday really is good news. It's the ending that lasts for ever.

CONNECTED TO HIS FOREVER ENDING

When Jesus rose from the dead, he was done with death and suffering and decay for ever. He broke through to a new life of joy and freedom.

And he did it for us. He did it as our representative so that we could share in his Sunday Ending.

You could imagine death as being like a brick wall which stands in our way. We're all heading straight for it. It brings our lives to a sudden end.

But Jesus has smashed a big hole in the wall, and all who are connected with him will pass safely through death to the forever life that is beyond.

We still live this side of the wall. We're still heading for death. We still face decay and frustration. We still cry and struggle.

But when we are connected with Jesus, the wall becomes a gateway to new life. His Sunday Ending becomes the end of our story.

Listen to how Jesus talks about it:

> *Very truly I tell you, whoever hears my word and believes him who sent me has eternal life and will not be judged but has crossed over from death to life.*
>
> John 5 v 24

Because Jesus has smashed through death, then so can we. Because Jesus has life for ever, then so can we.

We might be tempted to write this off as wishful thinking. I'd agree with you except that I'm convinced that Jesus rose from the dead. Actually, historically, absolutely. He really has smashed the hole that anyone can follow him through.

And life beyond the wall is a whole new life. Death will be done with; suffering will be over; there will be no more crying. Suddenly you discover that the Sunday Ending is actually a beautiful beginning.

It's hard to describe how wonderful a forever life with God will be—but here's a promise from the last book in the Bible that gives us some hints:

> *They will be his people, and God himself will be with*
> *them and be their God. He will wipe every tear from*
> *their eyes. There will be no more death or mourning*
> *or crying or pain, for the old order of things has*
> *passed away.*   *Revelation 21 v 3-4*

There will be eternal joy. There won't be a hint of sadness. We will all be perfect. It will be far beyond what we can imagine, and yet we will have real bodies and a new creation to explore and enjoy.

When C.S. Lewis wrote the stories of Narnia, he tried to capture this forever life. At the very end of the stories, as the main characters find themselves in a new and better world, he writes:

> *Now at last they were beginning Chapter One of the*
> *Great Story, which no one on earth has read; which*
> *goes on for ever; in which every chapter is better than*
> *the one before.*

And the forever life that we can have because of Jesus starts now.

As we experience day-to-day life with its various mini-endings, some happy and some sad, they are all transformed. When an ending is sad, we can look ahead to a time when there will be no more pain or sadness, and we can ask God to help us trust him in the meantime. And when an ending is happy, we can remind ourselves that an even happier ending is coming—one that will continue for ever—and we can thank God for that wonderful truth.

Jesus doesn't leave us to experience life's mini-endings on our own. God brought Jesus back to life at his Sunday Ending—and Jesus is still alive now. He gives his Spirit to everyone who trusts in him—guiding us, comforting us, and keeping us going through both happy mini-endings and sad mini-endings.

Because of Jesus, we can live happily ever after.

Making the **6** Connection

How does this connection between us and Jesus happen? Let's look again at how Jesus himself described it:

> *Very truly I tell you, whoever hears my word and believes him who sent me has eternal life and will not be judged but has crossed over from death to life.*
>
> John 5 v 24

Jesus said it involves two things. You *hear* his words, and you *believe*.

Jesus is the Creator, who has come in person so that we can know the life we were made for. We need to listen to him. We're surrounded by voices and ideas every day—people come and people go—but here's a voice unlike any other. Here's the voice of the God who made you.

Will you listen to him speak to you?

LISTEN TO JESUS

You can find out more as you read his story in the pages
of the Bible. Listen to what he says. Hear his promises.
A good place to start would be to read one of the four
Gospels—Matthew, Mark, Luke or John—which tell
the life story of Jesus.

And as you *hear* what Jesus says, then you need to
believe. That's the moment when the connection is
made. There isn't a ritual to perform or a test to pass.
You simply take Jesus at his word and say, "Yes, I
believe that you can give me this forever ending, and I'd
like you to do that for me".

At that moment you'll be connected to him. The
Friday Ending you deserve will be dealt with so that
beyond Friday you can enjoy the Sunday Ending you
were made for.

Here's a simple prayer that you could use to make that
connection right now:

Lord Jesus,

*I believe that you are my Creator. I'm sorry that I
have ignored you and broken the connection with you.
I know that I deserve a Friday Ending.*

*I find it amazing that you stepped into this world
and died for me. Thank you that on the cross you
took my Friday Ending. And thank you that you rose
again on Sunday.*

I want to share your Sunday Ending and live with you and for you for ever. Amen.

Or maybe you first want to find out more about Jesus and the Sunday Ending he offers. A good place to start would be to ask the person who gave you this book. They would be happy to talk with you or maybe to suggest a group where you could find out more.

Alternatively, go to the website christianityexplored.org, where you'll find video answers to questions about Jesus and what he offers. It will also show you whether there's a *Christianity Explored* or *Life Explored* course near you that you can join.

THE END

Our world is full of Friday Endings. But here's the ending that can give us hope and help us persevere.

Jesus was willing to share our Friday Ending, so that we could share His Sunday Ending.

This is the ending you were created for and the ending that will never disappoint you. This is the ending that will change your life for good.

thegoodbook
COMPANY

Thanks for reading this book. We hope you enjoyed it, and found it helpful.

Most people want to find answers to the big questions of life: Who are we? Why are we here? How should we live? But for many valid reasons we are often unable to find the time or the right space to think positively and carefully about them.

Perhaps you have questions that you need an answer for. Perhaps you have met Christians who have seemed unsympathetic or incomprehensible. Or maybe you are someone who has grown up believing, but need help to make things a little clearer.

At The Good Book Company, we're passionate about producing materials that help people of all ages and stages understand the heart of the Christian message, which is found in the pages of the Bible.

Whoever you are, and wherever you are at when it comes to these big questions, we hope we can help. As a publisher we want to help you look at the good book that is the Bible because we're convinced that as we meet the person who stands at its heart—Jesus Christ—we find the clearest answers to our biggest questions.

Visit our website to discover the range of books, videos and other resources we produce, or visit our partner site www.christianityexplored.org for a clear explanation of who Jesus is and why he came.

Thanks again for reading,

Your friends at The Good Book Company

thegoodbook.com | thegoodbook.co.uk
thegoodbook.com.au | thegoodbook.co.nz | thegoodbook.co.in
